CHALK TALK

CHALK TALK

An Analysis Of The Philosophies Of Oregon Football Coaches

Larry Geigle

COACHBEAR
BOOKS

Chalk Talk

A Thesis
Submitted to the
Department of Education and to
Linfield College
in Partial Fulfillment of the
Requirements for the Degree
Master of Education

Linfield College
McMinnville, Oregon
July 1978

CONTENTS

INTRODUCTION

In 1978 I received a master's degree from Linfield College, now known as Linfield University. One of the requirements was to write a thesis on a subject of your choice. At that time I was already a head football coach of a large middle school in Beaverton, Oregon. Picking my topic for the thesis was an easy choice. I decided to pick the minds of seven of the best football coaches in the area at that time. My thesis would focus on their football philosophies concerning offense, defense, and specialty teams. I also wanted to know what they looked for in players at different football positions. I would take the information and analyze it, then compare the answers. From my comparisons, I would discover likenesses and use the study to become a more knowledgeable and successful football coach. Interviewing these successful coaches was also going to be a rewarding experience.

The first coach I interviewed was Mouse Davis, who helped develop the run-and-shoot offense in high school, college, and in the pros. He is remembered for his high-powered offensive passing attack setting attendance records and points scored throughout the United States and Canada. Mouse has become a legend and has been inducted into the Oregon Athletics Hall of Fame. I played for Mouse at Sunset High School in Beaverton, Oregon. He was and always has been a dynamic personality. I can still remember his ability to light up our high school gym at Sunset, circling the gym on chariot pull by the cheerleaders dressed up as our mascot, the Apollo sun god, ready for battle. He was special to all of us students and players and a great example of positive energy. His teams were highly respected and well coached.

My second coach was John Allen from Jesuit High School in Beaverton, Oregon. John coached at Jesuit High from 1959 to 1977. His teams were always competing for the Oregon state title. Jesuit was listed as one of the top ten football teams in the state after their 1968 Oregon state championship. John went on to be inducted into the Jesuit High School Hall of Fame and was considered to be one of the best in the history of Oregon High School football. John Allen was known for his ability to get his teams ready for the big games. His pre-game locker room speeches were legendary. He was an exceptional student of the game and a wonderful educator. When his teams took the field, they were tough to beat.

The third coach was Wayne McKee, football coach at Beaverton High School in Beaverton, Oregon. Wayne McKee was the head junior varsity coach at Beaverton for a number of years under Duke Moore and John Lynn. His teams were highly successful, and his brand of football was rock solid. Even though Wayne was in the final years of his coaching career, his ideas about coaching football would be important information collected for this study.

I had the honor of coaching with Coach McKee after graduating from Linfield. He was a great man. He did not mince words and told it like it was. If you needed to play harder, he would let you know and his players would always respond. They always knew he was right! They believed in Coach McKee. He kept football simple for his players and pushed them to become successful. *A great coach!*

The fourth coach interviewed was from Sunset High School. Ron Linehan coached at Sunset High School in Beaverton, Oregon, from 1977 to 1993 and had a number of league titles. He was also the defensive coordinator at Sunset before becoming the head coach. The Sunset Apollos had won back-to-back state titles in 1975 and 1976 under Don Mathews. Don moved on to become a legend in the Canadian pro football league. When he left, Ron took over as head coach. After years at Sunset and many great teams, Ron became the head coach at Westview High School from 1994 to 2000. After retiring from teaching, he volunteered at Banks High School for the remainder of his coaching career. Ron was known to be a fierce competitor and a smart football coach. I was Ron's head freshman and head JV coach for two years. I got to see him in action up close. Ron was just plain tough as nails when it came to football. He was very well organized and expected his assistant coaches to carry their weight. While at Sunset, Ron's teams won a number of league titles and were always headed to the playoffs. His teams were well coached and ready to play. Coach Linehan implemented a long history of winning for Sunset's football program. I would stand on the field and watch Ron and I would say to myself, This guy is the real deal.

My fifth coach was again from Beaverton High School and a longtime assistant to Duke Moore. Duke passed away on the sidelines one Friday night of a heart attack and John Linn took over the program. He became the head coach in 1978. It only took Coach Linn three football season to win Beaverton High

School's first state football title. At that time I was the head coach at Highland Park Middle School, which fed players to Coach Linn's program at Beaverton High. The players passed on were big and talented. John and I watched together as these kids developed and grew into a real football powerhouse. We knew the group would be good and they were. They won the 1980 Oregon state football title. John was a dedicated teacher and football coach, and I enjoyed knowing and coaching with him. When I first came to Beaverton, John was the first coach to talk with me and let me know he was there if I needed any help. I realized Coach Linn knew so much about football—it was so frightening. When he was at up at the chalkboard drawing plays, if you didn't pay attention, John could leave you behind very quickly. He knew football and was also a wonderful dedicated teacher loved by the students and staff. I will always remember his love for the game.

The last coach I interviewed was Ted Henry, the offensive line coach at Linfield College. Ted was an outstanding line coach and spent his career helping to develop two outstanding football programs. The first was Hillsboro High School in Hillsboro, Oregon, as an assistant to Coach Ad Rutchman. After a number of years at Hillsboro and winning many league titles and the state football championship in 1966, Ad became the head football and baseball coach at Linfield College in 1969. Coach Henry was hired as his offensive line coach and offensive coordinator. Coach Henry remained with the program for many years, helping win two national college football titles. He coached at Linfield until his retirement. Later he was inducted into Linfield's Athletic Hall of Fame. I was fortunate to have played for Coach Henry at Linfield. He was loved and respected by everyone that knew him. Coach Henry was an example of an outstanding line coach and was a big part of the Linfield Wildcats' winning streak for over sixty years now. You knew as a player, Coach Henry must have been relentless on his blocking assignments. He was the perfect coach to prepare his players to win.

These coaches spent their lives developing young athletes and were the best of the best. It was great to have known them and be a part of their football programs. There is no doubt that the information collected in this study helped me to become a better football coach. I hope this book's readers will gain knowledge and wisdom from these great coaches of the past.

CHAPTER 1

Introduction

Coaches are becoming increasingly aware that coaching requires greater emphasis on communication, motivation, and the use of skilled techniques in developing good football teams. This increased awareness is evident by the highly competitive and skilled teams throughout Oregon today.

One of many ways a coach can improve in his knowledge and the use of new techniques is to attend numerous statewide coaching clinics. These clinics feature as speakers some of the most successful high school and college coaches in the nation today.

One other way of becoming a great coach is through many years of experience. This is where the true coach proves himself year after year, consistently developing winning teams. These coaches seem to have found the correct ingredients and combinations, not by chance or luck, but through dedication and hard work.

Purpose of the Study

The purpose of this study is to describe and analyze the coaching philosophies of successful football coaches in Oregon. After thoroughly understanding each of the philosophies, the investigator will prepare a comparison and summation of what these philosophies have in common. Others may then better understand what makes football coaches successful.

To better understand this study, the reader will need to understand what is meant by the term "coaching philosophy."

A philosophy in coaching comes about by many years of testing different methods and trying to receive a certain end result. When a coach uses one of these methods and finds a consistent winner, it becomes his football coaching philosophy.

Hypothesis

Certain specific, vital coaching techniques in skill, motivation, and communication are elements of a basic foundation in the philosophies of all great coaches. Even though different methods of implementation are employed, these philosophies are used, and the end result is the same: a winning team.

Procedures for the Study

1. Coaches who were selected for this study must have at least coached for ten years and have had at least five winning seasons.

2. All six coaches were personally interviewed with a tape recorder and the data placed in chapter 2 in written form.
3. All six coaches were asked the same ten questions, and only data pertinent to the study was retained.
4. Chapters 3 and 4 were then written, comparing likenesses and differences of the data.

Design of the Study

This study will be composed of three parts.

Part I.   A description of the philosophies of coaches in the area of techniques, communication, and motivation, collected through the following procedures:

    A. Personal interviews with successful football coaches in Oregon

    B. Using a questionnaire consisting of ten questions relating to the philosophies of the coaches and the result in techniques, communication, and motivation in football

Questions:

1. What is your offensive philosophy and why do you feel it is effective?
2. Please discuss what you would look for regarding offensive personnel and techniques of offensive personnel.
   a. Personnel
      1) split ends
      2) full backs
      3) half backs
      4) quarterbacks
      5) linemen
      6) centers

3. What is your defensive philosophy and why is it sound?

4. Please discuss what you would look for in personnel in the following defensive positions:
   1) linemen or tackles
   2) linebackers
   3) defensive ends
   4) defensive backs

5. Why is the kicking game important and what do you look for in a good kicking game?

6. Explain what you feel is important in your football practices.

7. What are your attitudes toward the following:
   a. training
   b. injuries
   c. scouting
   d. relations with players

Part II.   A summation of data pertaining to all coaching philosophies in reference to motivation, communication, and techniques through a comparison of similarities and differences.

Part III. The conclusion will identify philosophies that are very much alike and important to all coaches involved in the study. The study will also identify philosophies that differ among coaches and reveal why this is also true.

Definition of Terms

All nine definitions were taken from the Standard Encyclopedic Dictionary, Funk and Wagnall, J. G. Ferguson Publishing Company, 1972.

1. <u>Offensive Philosophy</u>: The inquiry into the most comprehensive principles of reality in offensive football regarding movement, attitude, or position of offense or attack.

2. <u>Offensive Technique</u>: The regarding of movement, attitude, or position for attack by using methods or manners of performance.

3. <u>Offensive Formation</u>: The regarding of movement, attitude, or position for players to attack by the act or process of forming or the state of being formed into different groupings.

4. <u>Running Attack</u>: The regarding of movement, attitude, or position for players who, by carrying the football, attempt to run through or around the line of the opposing team with aggressive physical contact.

5. <u>Offensive Passing Attack</u>: The regarding of movement or position for players who, by throwing the football, attempt to gain ground or yardage when a man on the same team receives the football downfield.

6. <u>Defensive Philosophy</u>: The inquiry into the most comprehensive principles in defensive football regarding the act of defending against an attack on your goal.

7. <u>Kick Game</u>: In football, to score (an extra point or a field goal) by kicking the ball.

8. <u>Training</u>: The state or condition of being trained in good health physically and mentally, along with study habits during the football season.

9. <u>General Rules</u>: Pertaining to, including, or affecting all or the whole football team with regulations or directions laid down by the coaches during football.

Related Philosophies

A review of the literature indicates a lack of research or analysis of different coaching philosophies in Oregon. There is a lack of the total picture for basic foundations to be used by young coaches. However, there have been a number of coaching books written, which give the coaches' personal viewpoints regarding coaching.

John McKay from the University of California looks at coaching as a way of life. He stresses to those who follow in his footsteps that coaching during a football season demands many hours a day. Coach McKay also motivates his players by giving them physical confidence as a very important ingredient.

Before Vince Lombardi died, he wrote a book that contained all areas of football that would be necessary to know about the game of football and what he felt could be understood by all.

Lombardi coached football for over thirty years, and he felt these areas were important to having good football teams. To the young player, it is an understanding that football is more than diagrams and techniques; it is a lot like life in its demands and commitments to excellence and to victory. Coach Lombardi points out, not only to players, but also to coaches, whatever the job we have, we must pay a high price for success.

CHAPTER 2

Questions Asked

Ten questions, which were used to determine the philosophies of football coaches and the result in techniques, communication, and motivation, are reported on in this chapter.

Question No. 1

1. What is your offensive philosophy and why do you feel it
   is effective?

Interview No. 1
Darrel "Mouse" Davis
Portland State Football

Basically our offensive philosophy is to attack the outside
perimeter and it is a skilled kids' offense. It is a quarterback's,
running back's and wide receiver's offense. Not that our
linemen don't enjoy it. They enjoy scoring and having great
success. In a skilled offense, you can attack the outside rather
than trying to beat people to death by running the football
up the middle or inside. We like to make the defensive teams
defense us outside because we put pressure on throwing the
ball first and that makes our running backs more effective.

This offense appeals to skilled kids because they can
practice the techniques all year around, or in the off-season.

Our offense also excites a lot of kids because it's a great
equalizer when your team is not great in size. This offense is
also a sound approach. I've been running it for fifteen years
so I really understand where to attack people.

If you run a running game, first you need a lot of help from
the crow's nest, but with our offense, you can see most of
what you need to see right from the ground.

We also try to make our running back more of a skilled kid
by letting him run to the open hole. I think also because it
is a fun offense—fun is moving the ball and scoring—we
have had good success. When talking about our skilled

kids, we're talking about any kid who is normally involved in running, throwing, and catching the football.

Our offense has set new attendance records. Even at a place like Hillsboro, we set new attendance records, so our offense is exciting to the public.

Interview No. 2
John Allen
Jesuit High School Football
Beaverton, Oregon

I have radically changed my offensive philosophy. I have really basically adopted the philosophy in which I have the best chance to win with. Looking at the kids that we have and the kids that I can see are coming in the future, the "run and shoot" offense seems to be the best chance for us.

I am not as locked into moving the football a certain way as I am in moving the ball. We know whenever you make a certain offensive thrust you must make a different defensive thrust. When we run a ball control offense, it is very important that we hold the defense from scoring.

The way it is now, we throw the ball a lot, and it is very likely we could score on the field from any place and at any time.

We do not feel it is essential that we hold people from scoring even though we would not like anyone to score on us. We can also throw two or three interceptions and not be hurt too badly.

What makes our offensive thrust work is this. We try to match up our strong people with their weak people in a creative way. If we can do this and find a weakness, we will score.

Interview No. 3
Wayne McKee
Beaverton High School Football
Beaverton, Oregon

I guess looking for balance in throwing the football, and also running the football. I feel if we can't do both and one just as good as the other, we're not successful. The idea behind offense is to move the ball. I don't think anyone can stop you if you do things right. I also feel one-half the game works for the other half. People can't play us for just one thing because we can throw and run, both the same.

Interview No. 4
Ron Linehan
Sunset High School
Beaverton, Oregon

We run the pro option offense. I would say that a balanced attack from the pro option is the best thing we've got going for us. It incorporates the triple option and puts a great amount of pressure on the defense along with pressure from the pro option passing attack. From there we can shift into an "I" formation, which gives us an inside look when running the ball.

We can always go back to our option if we need to go back

outside. We like to incorporate play action passes. We find these very effective in our offense and the straight dive play also. It's important for us to establish our running game up the middle and make the defense concerned about our inside game. If and when we do this, we find our outside game opening up for our option and also our play action passes.

We really believe in our play action passes at the high school level. We run our play action passes 70 percent of the time.

You've got to work with different formations, different sets also so that you can get the ball to the people you want to. It will really help the balance of your attack.

We try our hardest to attack the defense where there might be a weakness.

Interview No. 5
John Linn
Beaverton High School
Beaverton, Oregon

The first thing we must do here at Beaverton is to take our best players and build a defense. Then we can start looking for our offensive personnel.

Our offense must be able to sit on the ball and control it for long periods of time. We would like to be able to run from tackle to tackle and be effective. First we're going to run inside and then outside. After that we're throwing the football. If you take away our running game, then if we have to, we'll put the ball up fifteen times in a row. We believe our passing attack must be as good as our running game.

Interview No. 6
Ted Henry, Head Line Coach
Linfield College
McMinnville, Oregon

The offensive philosophy we've used here at Linfield for the past few years is to take advantage of other teams' weaknesses, along with being very versatile. Some games we may run the whole game just because that is our opponent's most serious weakness. We also carry a large offensive package with many different players that will fit the personnel we have that year. It is also important to us to work harder than other teams and try to perfect our offense and be consistent.

Question No. 2

2. Please discuss what you would look for in areas concerning different offensive personnel and techniques of offensive personnel.

(1) Mouse Davis – Portland State Football

Split ends come in a lot of different looks and sizes. You're looking for a kid that has good speed and can catch the football, and if the kid happens to be 5'8" or if he is 6'4" then he will be 6'4". A lot of kids here at Portland State have varied in size but have done the job. Receivers must have good hand-eye coordination. They must be able to concentrate on catching the football while being tackled. Split end patterns are much more disciplined, and he must know how to run square corners.

At fullback we look for a cross between a fullback and tailback. He's got to be a runner and also tough enough to block the corners. Our fullback has also become an important receiver the last couple of years.

I look for a quarterback at the high school level, not caring what his height is, but here at the college level, he must be a little taller to see over the defense. In our offense a quarterback's speed is not really a main factor. He must be able to throw the football well and have good leadership.

Our linemen need enough upper body strength to get on all fours and scramble. We do a lot of scramble-blocking. It's important in our offensive approach, and our kids need to have a great second effort, along with intelligence for consistency.

We look for a stable kid at center that you can bank on to do his job over and over again without mistakes. The center must be plugged into what's going on. We need a consistent effort from our center.

(2) John Allen – Jesuit High Football

Split ends must have speed in this position. They must be durable and able to catch the football in a crowd. They must know when they're open and to stop and catch the ball at that time.

Fullbacks need to be good blockers, number one. The fullback must be completely unselfish. The more running ability the fullback has, the better also.

The quarterback has three basic reads. One is the pre-snap read where he checks the alignment in the defensive backfield to understand if the other team is in a zone or man-to-man coverage. Two—the quarterback will drop-read—making a read as he drops back to pass. This read is also like a motion-read where you would send a man in motion and check how the defensive secondary reacts. Three—this is a set-read where the defense will try to hide the secondary coverage responsibilities by starting to roll and then going man-to-man. Once the quarterback has these three reads down, then the receivers can break their patterns according to the quarterback's movements. A quarterback must not necessarily have great speed, but more importantly, he should have quick feet. We can always improve a quarterback's arm if he has some ability in throwing the ball. I would also look for a kid with a calm temperament, a kid who has a positive expectancy of success. As a result of being calm in the contest, his perceptions and reactions are better and more relaxed. He must be able to perform in a game like he does in practice. A person who is tense or hyper is expecting defeat because he is seeing negative pictures of himself.

The slotbacks are our primary receivers. Through motion you can get a match-up. You can take your fastest guy and match him up with their slowest in a creative way, in the secondary. If you get a mismatch and get the completion, you will receive big dividends. Slotbacks need to be the fastest people. It's important that the slotback can run a disciplined pattern. He should also know when he is open and when he's found the open area and stop and catch the football.

Linemen – If in fact you can execute the offense and the linemen can tie up the opposing defensive line just for a few moments, then we can get the ball in the air. It's not really important that we beat linemen, but it is important to slow the defensive charge down. If you execute a pass offense efficiently when the other team has you outmanned, you stand a 50-50 chance of winning. If your personnel are evenly matched with the opponents, you stand a 60-40 chance of winning. If, however, you have better personnel, it's very likely you will win the contest.

Centers – Centers need to be really dependable and reliable. They must be highly predictable in what they do. You need a kid in this position who will do the same things over and over again.

(3) Wayne McKee, Beaverton High Football

Split End – This is a skilled position. You can't put just anyone at split end. He must be a kid who is disciplined in running his patterns. He must be a kid who learns rapidly where the zones and where the seams are. It takes a kid who can move and who is quick, not necessarily fast. He must have good hands and not be afraid to catch the football. You've also got to be able to block.

Running Backs – I don't believe a running back needs to be a great big kid. There are, however, certain things he must have. One is native speed. He must also have balance in a natural feel for running. You don't run all over the field. It's a very disciplined position. Good backs are born, not made. He must have guts because he knows he's the guy who is going to be tackled and must not be afraid to deliver a blow.

Quarterback – First thing that I would look for is leadership. If the kid has the receptiveness and the leadership, we can teach him the rest.

Tight ends – Number 1, the tight end is a blocker and receiving comes second. He must be able to block one-half of the double-team block or a secondary block. He must also be good at picking off the linebacker.

Linemen – Tackles are prime blockers and are important because they've got to be able to move the ball off tackle. They must be aggressive kids off the ball. Also, pass blocking is important. The tackle doesn't necessarily have to be your biggest kid, but he must have quick feet.

Guards are not as large as tackles, so they are able to pull and lead on traps and sweeps. They also must have quick feet.

Centers – The center must be a tough kid. We want a kid who can get off the line quickly and have a good exchange. We want a guy with a little height. Centers need to learn quickly about their position and that they must be aggressive and intelligent.

(4) Ron Linehan – Sunset High Football

Split Ends – There's definitely an ideal split end, but you don't really get a choice in high school for getting the ideal player. I've had split ends who were great, but not that fast. The one thing a wide receiver must have is concentration. He must be intelligent, and this intelligence helps him learn how to get open and where. The rest of it is timing—making the cut. Our kids also attend football camps together.

Backs – You would like to have your backs both inside and outside runners. We put our quickest back to the weak side and the strong back to the strong side so our quick back gets outside and our strong back runs well inside. We really think speed is important with our backs.

Quarterbacks – We look for a kid who can throw the ball a great distance. The short routes are also very important to our passing attack. He must be adequate at running the option. He needs to be a leader in some respects, but because we call all our plays, there is not that much pressure on our quarterback.

Linemen – The weak tackle doesn't have to be the best drive blocker in the world. He must, however, be quick and still have good blocking techniques. Strong tackles must be big and excellent drive blockers. They must be able to secure the inside running attack and also secure the defensive tackles when we run outside. They can be lacking in some areas, but must be able to move people out. Guards trap a lot and must be able to move with mobility and agility to get the job done. They must be able to get up and get off the ball or line of scrimmage.

Centers – Our centers must be able, number one, to get the ball up, and then they must be able to secure the defensive middle guard.

(5) John Linn – Beaverton High School

Split End – Our split ends must be able, number one, to catch the ball and have consistency. They probably aren't that great as blockers.

Backs – Beaverton backs must be quick and able to act to avoid tackles. Our backs don't have to be big or good blockers.

Quarterback – The quarterback must be quick and coachable. We want to throw the football, and we also feel we can teach him to do this. We want him able to run the option. The quarterback must be intense and see himself doing the job.

Offensive Linemen – The linemen must be the smartest people on the team because of their line calls. All linemen must get off the ball quick. Tight ends must be good blockers first and catch the football second.

Center – We like our centers to be tall for a good exchange between the quarterback and center. Centers need also to be consistent and disciplined.

(6) Ted Henry, Linfield College

Tight Ends – Basically we want someone who can block. He needs also to be able to catch a pass, but blocking is number one.

Offensive Line – All our linemen have good, quick feet. Tackles do not have to be as mobile as the guards. Hitting and maintaining contact with your man is one of our most important goals. Guards need to pull well, and all linemen must be good pass blockers.

Centers – The center must be consistent and a good blocker especially on the middle-linebacker. Centers have the number one job of starting the play the same way every time.

Split Ends – The number one thing we search for in our split end is the ability to catch the football and then, also, to block downfield and on the line of scrimmage.

Fullbacks – We want our fullbacks, number one, to block and then to obtain the short gain of two or three yards when we need it.

Halfbacks – Our halfbacks must be able to block and catch the ball as well as break a run for the long yardage.

Quarterback – Quarterbacks come in different abilities.

We are fortunate to have a quarterback who can sprint-out pass, drop-back pass and run the football.

Question No. 3

3. What is your defensive philosophy and why is it sound?

(1) Mouse Davis – Portland State Football

First thing we do is try and start with a defensive philosophy that is sound. A defense in which you can cover all defensive situations and your rules for these defenses are sound also. It really doesn't matter if it's a 5-2 or 4-3 defense. Then, when this has been done and you stunt and blitz, you already know where your weaknesses are going to be. It's also important that one kid doesn't do forty-three different things on defense. I do have one other defensive philosophy and that is pursuit. Anything that will help your players get to the football faster is important. To stand people up on defense might have a tendency to make your defense soft. Even though it might give you quicker pursuit. Also, we believe in having great enthusiasm toward the game.

A defensive coach needs to find a sound defense first, then players who like to play with a little more emotion than offensive players.

(2) John Allen – Jesuit High School

Our first principle or goal is to prevent the touchdown. You do "not want to overlook the statistics on defense" and how effective a defense really is. An evenly matched defensive team will deliver a blow to each other, driving both teams up and down the field. The goal or objective is, even though you are driven back, don't ever be scored upon.

Defensively there are five ways to score, while there are only three on offense. Defensively you can score on an intercepted pass, punt return, or a recovered fumble, and then you may also score on a safety or blocked punt. If either team can drive its opponent down to the goal line, the chances of scoring by one of the five methods mentioned above becomes a real threat, and many times they will win the ballgame.

To have the opposing team's offensive thrust backfire delivers a severe blow to their morale and could possibly lead to a total collapse. At the same time you provide a lift for your team and often this turns a closely contested game into a runaway.

There are three basic theories of line defense. One is to read and react from a basic key. Another is to penetrate and read the play as it develops, and the third is to blitz. All of these have four basic techniques involved. They are alignment, key, attack, and neutralize. We believe there is a fifth dimension that we can use. The hole technique as a primary line of attack. We concentrate on one area to attack the offense. Then, after the ball carrier commits himself in a direction by following our penetration keys, we hope to converge on the ball carrier through relentless pursuit.

Our goal is to keep the gain to a minimum and prevent the long touchdown run or pass. Whenever it's a short yardage situation such as a goal line situation, we will employ a special defense with the emphasis being line defense.

If it is a pass, we would like to destroy the pass or the timing of the offensive play. Our defensive backs should be able to cover their receivers close because of the pressure from the front seven.

Defense is essentially tackling and pursuit of the ball carrier. You must also have your defense coordinated for situations that will come about. If you're going to blitz or stunt on defense, you will need a great second effort after the first movement. Defense is also a team thing. There is no other way to achieve success if your defense is a lot of individuals doing their own things. If this happens, your defense will break down for sure. A thinking ballplayer is also a stinking ballplayer. He should be able to react on instinct or repetition from practice.

(3) Wayne McKee, Beaverton High School Football

Mobility and the willingness to strike. Pursuit is very important to keep people from turning the corners for the big gainers. I've found that it's not really how big your players are, but how quick they can be, and are they willing to tackle or strike hard.

(4) Ron Linehan, Sunset High School Football

Defensively, we are very basic technique-wise. We try to give the kid a good concept of the game. If you've got a kid who can read what an offensive lineman is going to do, you're teaching the concept of football, and we like to do that. It's very important to us to teach our kids about the game of football and why people do certain things, and once they understand, they become real football players. The reason we do well is because we play defense touch all the way down the field. We are basically a pretty honest defensive team, but spend a lot of time on perfecting our techniques. The kids believe in it and have had success with our defense. Our kids also know if they get better at their techniques, the better the game will go on Friday night.

We key up on the defense in different situations and use our different techniques to get the job done.

(5) John Linn – Beaverton High School

Defensive philosophy – Our philosophy is "give but don't break." We want the opposing ball club to drive us all the way down the field without a mistake. It's tough to do this, and most teams will make a mistake. Your defense must not break down for long yardage. We try to take away your big play. All defenses have weaknesses, and coaches need to know this. Pursuit is also important as is intensity.

(6) Ted Henry – Linfield College

We believe in a total team defense concept. Everyone must do his job; first the fly to the football and make the tackle. Defensive players must be disciplined enough to play team defense. Our goal is to hit quick and react to the ball carrier with great pursuit. We also need aggressive players and be able to deliver a good strike.

Question No. 4

4. Please discuss what you would look for in personnel in the following defensive positions:
    a. defensive tackle
    b. linebacker
    c. defensive ends
    d. defensive backs

(1) Mouse Davis – Portland State Football

Defensive Tackles – Most of our defensive linemen must be over 210 pounds or they are considered too small. Our defensive line must go against kids that weigh between 260 and 270. It's important that we have fair size so we're not blown off the ball. They must be able to pass rush and pursue the ball carrier.

Defensive Linebackers – Our linebackers are big, but not so big as to lose quickness and pursuit. They are the defensive captains and must be very intense in what they try to do. Our linebackers are strikers and, most of all, great tacklers.

Defensive Ends – Our defensive ends must be good at containing the outside run and also helping out inside. Their largest job is taking on the fullbacks' blocks or the halfbacks' blocks.

Defensive Backs – These kids must be very quick and not make the mistake of getting beaten deep. They've also got to come up and stop the outside game as well as the inside game if there is a breakdown by our defense.

(2) John Allen – Jesuit High Football

Defensive Tackle – These are big players who like physical contact and just plain like to hit people. They must have good pass rush techniques along with tackling techniques.

Linebackers – A good linebacker is the player you wouldn't want your daughter to date.

Defensive Backs – These players must have quick feet and must be tough, but also a little frightened.

Defensive Ends – These guys are somewhat like defensive backs, but like physical contact also. The defensive end is a kind of counter-puncher.

(3) Wayne McKee – Beaverton High Football

Defensive Tackle – We have found, using the radar defense, you really don't need size and the kids really like the defense. It enables your defensive line to miss most of the physical contact and make the tackle without getting beat up so much. I prefer a kid who is quicker over a larger player. Using the radar, we find our defensive linemen getting to the football quicker. He doesn't need to be big, but quick and a good tackler.

Linebackers – They must be strikers or good tacklers. They must be disciplined and respected by the rest of our team for leadership. There are times and situations in which they are key personnel and must be there when needed. The linebacker must not be afraid to meet the blocker and also be able to read keys effectively. Quickness is important and pursuit is vital.

Defensive Backs – We would like to have tall kids here, if possible, because they seem to have a better success percentage. We don't always have tall kids, but we would like to. This player must have better-than-average speed and must be very disciplined reading pass first then run. If he does read run, he must react quickly enough to stop a big gainer.

Defensive Ends – My defensive ends are always taught two-thirds inside and one-third outside responsibility unless we're playing the option or some uncommon offense. Our defensive end also always works in defensive teams with the corners and safeties. Quickness is also important here as well as the ability to take on the blocker.

(4) Ron Linehan – Sunset High Football

Defensive Tackle – The defensive line must be quick and have a great attitude. They have to accept what we do totally. The defensive line feeling is one of power. The linebackers have a leadership feeling. Defensive backs have a lot of public pressure. It's harder to play defensive line without mistakes than it is other positions. You've got to teach technique and reaction.

Defensive Linebackers – Our linebackers must be good leaders and help run our defensive ball club. We feel it's important to have good tacklers and pass defenders at this position.

Defensive Backs – Defensive backs must be quick and not make a mistake because if they do, it's six points. The public sees everything they do, right or wrong.

Defensive Ends – Defensive ends must secure the outside running game and then the inside game if we're playing the option. Defensive ends must also be quick and good tacklers.

(5) John Linn – Beaverton High

Defensive Personnel – Our best four defensive players are our defensive backs. These players must have good quickness. They must have good techniques. Free safety must be a center fielder—the corners need to be able to fill on the running plays.

Linebackers – The quick side linebacker must be able to move quickly. The strong side linebacker is not as quick but needs to be able to stop the run inside.

Defensive Ends are quick and are hitters and must keep their heads glued on. They are head hunters.

Tackles are big and good readers. They must have a good pass rush and help with the run outside.

(6) Ted Henry – Linfield College

Defensive Personnel – Secondary players would like to be quick and have great speed. This is not a must, however, to being in the secondary. This player must also be a good tackler, fill on the run, and never get beaten deep.

Linebackers – Linebackers must stress good techniques taking on the fullbacks and other blockers. They must be quick and extremely good hitters.

Defensive Ends must protect the run outside and in our philosophy are almost the same as linebackers, being mobile and good hitters.

Question No. 5

5. Why is the kicking game important and what do you look for in a good kicking game?

(1) Mouse Davis – Portland State Football

Not this year, but the year before last, we lost three ballgames. We could have won all three of them if we had been superior in the kicking game. I think we work hard on this part of our game. We break our kicking game down on film and evaluate it piece by piece. If the game is close, the kicking game is an edge and can win it for you. If you can win the kicking game and the offensive part of the game, or else the kicking game and the defensive part of the game, then you have won two out of the three needed for victory. We work on it and we do enough different things that people are going to have to respect us for what we do with our kicking game.

(2) John Allen – Jesuit High School

The kind of offense you run along with the kind of defense all have a direct influence on your kicking game and how important it will be to you. If you have a power control offense, then it's very likely you would want a good punt and punt return team to keep the opponents as far away from your goal as possible.

If you were an explosive football team, the punter would probably punt the ball out of bounds more because punting is not that important as far as field position goes.

There are many factors that go into the kicking game. The punting game is very important in that if you get a successful punter, you can move the football many times just by punting. If you can also get a kickoff man who can consistently kick the ball between the 10- to 23-yard lines low, you might just as well gamble on an onside kick. You can bet the opponent will run the ball back between the 30- to 45-yard lines. Unless I've got a kicker who can kick the ball inside the 10-yard line I'm for using some unorthodox type of kickoff. Because of the fact, they can return the ball quicker.

The most effective kickoff return is to get a kid who will attack the opponent and pop it the way you would on a dive play. The return man is the single most important person. When developing a kickoff man, you're looking for the kid who has rhythm just like you would in a punter. The two things such as rhythm and a natural ability to kick the ball are needed for a kickoff specialist. We like only a few people to help our kickers so they don't have too many things to think about at one time. I'm not really sure you can develop a kicker unless he has a natural ability.

It's very important to remember to have a good kickoff team and that they are well balanced and cover the whole field on a kickoff. The kicking game should be practiced one-fifth of the time you have for practice. I hate to see a ball fair-caught and roll twenty extra yards when the kid decides not to catch it. I like my players to step up and catch the ball. It's important to try and get as much as you can.

There are definite things in the kicking game you must commit yourself to. Sometimes the weather conditions play an important factor in your kicking game. Some teams feel the quick kick is a very effective tool. The kicking game must be practiced to have real success, and because your kicking game is good, you're able to win games you should maybe have lost.

(3) Wayne McKee – Beaverton High Football

I feel that it is one more part of the football game. It's important to work on your kicking game every practice. In our kicking game, we like our people who can get downfield quickly and who are good open field tacklers. If one of our kicks are blocked, it's a downright sin. Being able to return the football is important, and finding and teaching correct blocking assignments on returns is important also. We would like to block at least one kick a game.

(4) Ron Linehan – Sunset High Football

We spend a great amount of time on the kicking game. In our regular season we may not punt the ball more than six times, but still we work hard on that part of the game because we know how important it is. There are situations when you really need the kicking game for field position.

(5) John Linn – Beaverton High Football

The kicking game is very important to the final outcome of the football game. If you can get a punter to punt the ball down the field, you can move yourself into great field position. Covering kickoffs and punts are important to get people down the field and tackle the ball carrier. You must work on the kicking game 20 to 30 percent of your practice.

(6) Ted Henry – Linfield College

We believe, in order to win a football game, we must win two out of three of these areas: offense, defense, or the kicking game. We spend many hours trying to perfect our kicking game and pick up the hidden yardage gained by a good punter or return man. We must know our personnel and what they can do.

Question No. 6

6. Give a general idea what is important in your football practices.

(1) Mouse Davis – Portland State Football

Our warm-up in practice has always been relaxed. I think being relaxed is the best way to get your offensive kids ready to work. Even a little thing like warm-up is so important to analyze what you are.

I think being disciplined just to be disciplined is bad. But to have a reason for doing it is good. It's not our way to be disciplined in warm-ups so we don't do that particular thing.

You really need to break your practice down across the field. We don't a lot because we feel it's better to teach in practice and hit in the games. We try to avoid injuries. The first part of the season we hit well, more depending on experience. During our tackling drills and blocking drills, we well hit, but we only scrimmage live time before our season opens.

I really think you can over-practice and under-practice. Sometimes coaches get so excited about over-practicing they under-practice. That is something you have to feel out on your own. Your players should always want to hit in the ballgames.

(2) John Allen – Jesuit High Football

The more organized your practices are, in the sense that you have a maximum number of repetitions practiced. What and why is very important. You have a teaching period and you teach things to help players develop certain skills, then after your players have these skills mentally, you set up a situation of a maximum number of repetitions. We have a saying that "a thinking football player is a stinking football player."

There is such a thing as practicing too much or too long. There is a limit to how much kids can take in. If you came upon a situation which puts you the underdog, then you'll probably have to take more time in practice.

(3) Wayne McKee – Beaverton High Football

Nothing you do should be done too long. You should spend equal time with offense and defense. Equal time also between line play and backfield play. Drills become very important to my practice plan. You don't want to, however, stay in one drill too long. There should be a certain time each practice where the team gets together and talks about what is happening, so everyone understands where the team is and why. I've never believed in practices on weekends, but it seems a lot of people do it now. Players need to enjoy time to themselves during the season.

(4) Ron Linehan – Sunset High Football

You can't change the practices, so you won't bore kids. If you're so good at something that you don't think you should do it anymore, then you're getting to be a pretty good football team. Any time you think you've taught a skill to some high point, then you let up, you're on your way to a new low.

The level of concentration is very important to our practices. Kids must be intelligent to play for us. We try and sell the kids. You must be better today and every day.

(5) John Linn – Beaverton High Football

In our practices, it's important not to have any wasted time on the field. You must plan what you're going to do and stick with it. We try and break down our practices into different time areas. It's important to do this because there is less time wasted. We don't believe in talking on the field. The players shouldn't be standing around wasting time. If players are standing around, our practices will probably be too long. Repetition is important to good practices. There must be a great amount of repetition. All drills used in practices should be there to make better football players.

(7) Ted Henry – Linfield College

> Organization is the most important ingredient to a
> successful practice and the ability to work harder than
> other teams. Players shouldn't be standing around wasting
> time and having a lot of coaches really helps. Working
> toward perfection is a major goal at Linfield and a tradition
> has been set up over the years for winning.

Questions No. 7–10

What are your attitudes toward the following:

(1) Davis – Portland State Football

> <u>Training</u> – Rules on drinking, smoking, and other things
> bad must be firmly dealt with. In college, we try and treat
> the players like men and your attitude is different than it
> is in high school.

> You must have discipline. People sometimes look at
> discipline as a good method of being firm. The players
> need to be disciplined enough to do things we need to do.

<u>Injuries</u> – Any time a player is injured, we want to know. He must check with a coach or trainer.

<u>Relationships with Players</u> – You've got to be able to understand what you want to do, then convey that to the player in the easiest manner. You will have success or failures by the rapport you have with your players. Anything you can do for your players off the field, as well as on the field, is part of your job.

<u>Scouting</u> – The best method for us, besides secret phone calls, are previous game films. We can break them down and really study what teams are doing.

(2) John Allen – Jesuit High Football

<u>Training</u> – It's really hard to force kids not to drink. I don't want it to happen, but it's hard these days, with all the different commercials on television with players drinking and doing their own thing. We dislike it at this level.

We agree as a group that certain things will benefit the team and that other things will not. We want the kids to agree on these training rules and help enforce them. If a player is caught, there will be certain consequences he will have to face.

<u>Playing Personnel</u> – We would like to play everyone. If I have good enough people, I can play everyone.

<u>Injuries</u> – We have had very few injuries. I also provide the best possible staff of doctors if a player is hurt. I want to know about all injuries.

<u>Scouting</u> – Films are the most successful for us because we can break them down.

<u>Relationships with Players</u> – I try to do as much as I can for my players so they can respect me now and ten years from now.

(3) Wayne McKee – Beaverton High Football

<u>Training</u> – Kids do things differently today than when I was at that age. We work hard in trying to instill loyalty to our teams and even though some kids don't really understand why it is so important to our way of thinking.

We're going to also let them know that if we catch one of our players breaking the standards we've set down, they will face certain consequences. It's important to us that players make all practices and that the last thing we want to do is kick a player off the team.

<u>Playing Personnel</u> – I try to get as many people in the ballgame as I can. If we have a game that is close, then we feel, by the time a player is fifteen years of age, he should know the difference between a starter and a substitute.

<u>Injuries</u> – We want to know about all injuries. I never will play youngsters who are hurt, and if they don't tell me, I get upset if they're hurt.

<u>Public Relations</u> – Players must understand and get to know their coach. I want to be friendly and have the kids know they're welcome to talk with me at any time, but on the field I want to be firm and fair to everyone equally. I think it's important to criticize the whole ball club and not

just one person in front of everyone else. I try to set very high standards.

My assistant coaches must be loyal and have their own personalities. I like them to feel they are coaching their areas and that they can coach them well. I don't want my assistant coaches changing things without me knowing.

Scouting – I think everybody is using films because you can break them down and see what is happening. I don't believe it will ever take place of the team actually being seen in a live situation.

(4) Ron Linehan – Sunset High School Football

Training – We have a set of rules to abide by and which are required by the district. Anyone caught smoking or drinking is off the team.

Injuries – We want to know about all injuries and treat them as serious.

Relationships with Players – You don't get the full value of coaching unless you are close to your players. You may have a chance to help the kid in a way his parents cannot.

(5) John Linn – Beaverton High Football

Training – When we discuss training, with our players, there are four things important:
- a. family
- b. school
- c. church
- d. football team

We tell the kids not to do anything that would embarrass these four areas.

<u>Injuries</u> – When one of our players is injured, we never play him in a ballgame. If he doesn't practice Tuesday or Wednesday, he won't play on Friday.

<u>Scouting</u> – Our scouting consists of the punch system with punch cards and breaking down game films. From our films, we can find personnel weakness, offensive blocking assignments, and defensive alignments.

<u>Relationships with Players</u> – The relationship with the player is the most important thing in coaching. If I didn't enjoy doing it, I wouldn't be here. You don't have to be their best friend, but you need to communicate with them.

(6) Ted Henry – Linfield College

<u>Training</u> – We don't want our players drinking, smoking, or embarrassing the team in any way. We don't believe these things are going to help students play football better.

<u>Injuries</u> – We like to have good doctors available to help with injuries in practice, as well as in games. It eliminates any doubts we might have about playing a player.

<u>Scouting</u> – We use films and break them down offensively and defensively. We would also like to study a team in person.

<u>Relationships with Players</u> – My players are important to me. I hope they respect me, not necessarily like me. I think most of them do respect what I know and I haven't really asked if they've cared about me.

CHAPTER 3

Philosophy Comparisons

Using the ten questions related to the offensive philosophies of the coaches interviewed and their techniques, a comparison of like philosophies will be made.

1. What is your offensive philosophy and why do you feel it is effective?

When comparing all six coaches for likenesses in their offensive philosophies, we find five basic similarities. First, all six coaches agreed that the number one thing of importance in an offense is to move the football.

"Mouse" Davis of Portland State stated that his kids have a high degree of success because they are able to move the football and score many touchdowns in a single game. Davis uses the "run and shoot" offense.

John Allen of Jesuit High School also uses the "run and shoot" philosophy. He feels his kids must be able to score from any place and time on the football field to realize success.

Wayne McKee says the idea behind offense is to move the football. If you do the things right for a good offensive thrust, no one can stop you from moving the ball. Even though Coach McKee of Beaverton High doesn't use the run and shoot like Davis or Allen, he still understands that the football must move.

Coach Linehan from Sunset High School illustrates his concern for moving the football by putting a number one priority on running the football up the middle. If we can do this, Linehan feels, it will open up our offense outside and our play action passes as well as our pro option passing attack.

The second area in which the four previously mentioned coaches agreed was balance in their offensive attack.

Davis tries to attain balance by throwing the ball to his opponent's outside perimeter and then coming back up the middle with his fullback.

Allen of Jesuit tries to match up his strong players with the other team's weak players. This, in a sense, creates a balance in favor of Allen's Crusaders. The opposing defensive teams try to stop or find the mismatch by changing their defensive game plan and, in turn, it opens up other areas that become weak.

Wayne McKee believes very strongly you must throw the football as well as you run the football in creating balance. McKee also stated that the passing game works in turn for the running game, and if you depend on one of these by itself, you will create an imbalance. It is important to McKee that other teams must defend more than just one phase of offensive football.

Sunset's Linehan feels that a balanced attack from the pro option is very much a part of his offensive philosophy. We incorporate the triple option running attack, which puts a great amount of pressure on the defense, along with the triple option passing attack. From this point, we shift into our "I" formation and run the ball up the middle, and this gives us an offensively balanced attack.

The third area all six coaches have in common agreement is to attack a certain area or weakness.

Davis feels the best and quickest way for the offense to score is to throw the ball to the outside perimeter, creating a weakness inside for his fullback.

Allen tries to align his strong ballplayers up with the weak players on the defense in a creative way to make a mismatch.

Wayne McKee and Linehan start off by trying the middle with their running game and finding the defense's weakness. When the weakness is strengthened, then other areas of the opposing defense become vulnerable.

The fourth area in which the coaches have all agreed is the

running or passing attack and how important it is to establish one to help the other.

Davis tries to establish a passing attack first and then a running attack. He feels they can do this against anyone if his backs and ends run their patterns correctly.

Allen feels that the passing attack is a number one priority in his run and shoot. He feels they must try and also run outside for the big gainer.

McKee from Beaverton again feels it is important to move the ball by establishing a running game first and then a passing game—doing both well.

Sunset's Coach Linehan gets his triple option moving number one, which is a combination inside and outside running attack and then employs his passing attack. If he can get the running attack going up the middle and it draws the defense to that particular area, then the passing and play action passing is wide open.

In this study, the final or fifth way all coaches seem to be in agreement is this. They would all like the other teams to defend them in a certain manner. Davis wants teams to defend him to the outside. Allen would like their weak players on his strong. McKee felt that no team could defense just one phase of his offense, and Sunset's Linehan develops such a strong running game that a defense has no choice but to try and keep the middle closed up.

2. Please discuss what you would look for in areas concerning different offensive personnel and techniques of offensive personnel.

When comparing all six coaches' preferences in their split ends, fullbacks, quarterbacks, linemen and centers, we find these basic similarities:

Concerning the split end position on offense, all six coaches agreed on these basic considerations. First, not all good split ends are one particular size or shape. Secondly, it is important, number one, that they have quickness and speed if possible. Thirdly, all split ends should have good hand-and-eye coordination in catching the football. Fourthly, concentration in catching the football while being tackled in a crowd and, lastly, split ends should be able to run disciplined patterns and square corners.

Making a comparison of the fullback position, these ideas concerning a good fullback were agreed upon.

The fullback must have first good speed, according to all six coaches. Secondly, he must be able to run the ball inside or up the middle for good yardage. Then, lastly, the coaches, when interviewed, felt that the fullback must be an unselfish blocker.

Looking at the quarterback position, there was a wide variety of needs, but the coaches did agree that all quarterbacks must have leadership ability and be able to throw the football. Davis and Allen emphasized this more because their particular offenses move the ball through the air by throwing.

Linemen have these basic needs of similarity. First, all linemen must have quickness to get started after the ball is hiked. There was also agreement that a lineman must be a great blocker on running plays and on passing plays. Davis and Allen both were in agreement that a lineman in their offenses didn't really need to beat the opponent, but did need to tie him up so that he could not pursue the quarterback before he has the chance to throw the football.

Sizing up the centers, it was vital to realize the importance of this position. A center needs to have intelligence, be consistent and highly predictable. He must also be able to move quickly after the ball is hiked. It was in agreement that the center's number one job is to get the football to the quarterback without making a mistake when the ball is hiked.

The backs are important to the offensive thrust of any offensive team. All six coaches agree that the backs who are great have a natural talent in speed, agility, and coordination of their bodies.

3.   What is your defensive philosophy and why is it sound?

After talking with the six coaches interviewed, these points were brought out and agreed upon.

Defensive players seem to do better if they play with more emotion than do offensive players, who normally would rather show consistency rather than emotion. According to all six coaches, a defense must have pursuit and the ability to strike hard. The coaches also mentioned that defense is a team function and if one player breaks down, it can cause many weaknesses because other players may try to overcompensate for the mistake. Defenses must prevent the long gainer and make the opponent work hard all the way down the field to score. No matter whether a defense is 5-3 or 4-3, it doesn't matter as long as the defense is sound. The coaches wanted to point out that when running a stunt, you automatically realize and create weaknesses in your defense and you should not blame a player if, because of stunting, the opposing team makes a long run. Another area concerning defense is that which teaches the player the whole concept of defense, not just his job. Linehan, Henry and Allen stress this when talking about reading keys or knowing where to go and what to do by what the offensive line is doing, whether it be pass, play action pass, or run. It was also agreed on that the defense must get to the passer and destroy the quarterback or his timing.

4. Please discuss what you would look for in personnel in the following defensive positions:
   a. defensive tackles
   b. linebacker
   c. defensive ends
   d. defensive backs

When comparing all six coaches for similarities in their defensive tackles, linebackers, defensive ends and defensive backs, we find these areas in agreement.

All six coaches feel that their defensive tackles must be big and strong. Secondly, they must be good pass rushers and have good quickness so there is no chance of being blown back by the offensive linemen's charge. All defensive tackles should love physical contact and be good tackles.

When discussing linebackers, coaches really feel the player should have great pursuit after the ball carrier, along with being a good tackler. They must also be very deliberate about what they would like to accomplish on defense.

All six coaches agreed that a defensive end must have good outside run containment so the running back with the ball will not break loose. The defensive end needs also to help inside on running plays. He should like physical contact and be able to take on the blocker.

5. Why is the kicking game important, and what do you look for in a good kicking game?

When discussing the kicking game with all six coaches, these areas were in agreement and very important.

The kicking game should, number one, be worked on every day in practice. Your opponents must respect what your kicking game can do to them. Secondly, if a football game is close, then your kicking can be the edge to winning. Thirdly, the coaches felt that many times during a season, you can acquire good field position by a long punt or kickoff.

When the coaches were asked what is important to defense against a good kicking game, these points were agreed upon. The defenders must be able to get downfield quickly in order to make a good tackle. It is important that they cover the whole field and have a good pursuit angle as tacklers.

When looking for a kicker the coaches felt, number one, that the player should be a natural kicker and have good rhythm.

The players catching punts and kickoffs are very important. They should have good hands and speed to catch the ball and run through the holes on kickoff and punt return. The players who receive should also be good at fair catches.

6. Give a general idea what is important in your football practices.

The coaches felt that disciplined practices are an important ingredient to winning football games. Breaking down each practice session, making sure it is organized and well run today and tomorrow. Using drills that do not take too long, but have a high degree of repetition relating to a football situation. Some coaches also practice too long and others not long enough, according to the interviews. A high level of concentration is needed in a football practice.

7.   What are your attitudes toward the following areas – <u>Training</u>?

All coaches felt that rules dealing with smoking, drinking, and bad habits should be dealt with firmly. Discipline was important to the training concept for players, along with the matter of the coach being firm.

8.   What are your attitudes toward the following areas – <u>Injuries</u>?

The coaches wanted to know about all injuries so players could be treated properly. Playing when you are injured, they agreed, was not a good idea.

9.   What are your attitudes toward the following areas – <u>Relationships with Players</u>?

Communication was vital with all coaches, along with helping the players in other areas of maturing. Being able to convey or stress a particular idea to the player was also a high priority with the six previously mentioned coaches.

10. What are your attitudes toward the following areas – <u>Scouting</u>?

All six coaches use films for their scouting. They feel it is a good method to help break down what the opponent is trying to do. It was also felt to be important, however, to see the team in live action and realize what the team feeling was.

CHAPTER 4

Philosophy Differences

Using the ten questions related to the offensive philosophies of the coaches interviewed and their techniques, a comparison of differences in philosophies will be made.

1. What is your offensive philosophy and why do you feel it is effective?

When comparing all six coaches' philosophies concerning offense, we find these differences.

Coach Davis of Portland State felt that his offense appeals to many sports fans because it is exciting. Davis also felt, because of fifteen years of past experience running the "run and shoot," that this helps win ballgames. The fact that his teams have set new attendance records does not hurt either when trying to draw new players from high schools and junior colleges.

John Allen had many different ideas relating to his belief in a good offensive philosophy. Allen runs the offense he feels he has the best chance of winning with. Also, when making a certain offensive thrust, you need to come back with a particular defensive thrust to balance your whole attack. Allen does not want anyone to score, but does not feel badly if they do. His offense scores a lot of touchdowns a game, so it is not important to shut the opposing team out.

Wayne McKee really didn't have a different idea, at least in this area. His offense is very solid and sound, along with being well-balanced.

Sunset's Coach Linehan feels very strongly that play action passes are a real advantage to his offensive philosophy. He also feels that using a variety of formations to make sure you are getting the ball to your strongest players is important.

John Linn of Beaverton feels it is important to keep your offense simple and not give his players too much pressure to contend with.

Ted Henry at Linfield uses a large offensive package, and the coaches pick what will be useful for that particular year by what their personnel can do.

2. Please discuss what you would look for in areas concerning different offensive personnel and techniques of offensive personnel.

When comparing the philosophies of all six coaches for differences in their split ends, fullbacks, quarterbacks, linemen, and centers, we find these basic differences:

Split Ends

Davis didn't really point out any differences and Allen, McKee, and Linehan all had the same needs in their split ends as did Linn and Henry.

Fullbacks

Davis felt the difference in his fullback is that he looks for a cross between a tailback and a fullback because this position requires catching numerous passes. Coach Allen didn't discuss any differences in this area. McKee from Beaverton High School believes balance is needed to be a great fullback. McKee also felt courage is vital to being a good ball carrier. Coach Linehan had no differences in this area. Linn and Henry had no differences.

Quarterback

Davis felt this: his quarterback must be tall in order to read defenses. Allen felt it was important to teach three reads step as quarterback. One is the pre-snap read. Two is the drop-read and three the set-read. All three needed in becoming a good quarterback. Allen also felt that the quarterback must have a good positive self-image. He must be able to function in a ballgame, like he does in practice, and still be poised. McKee and Linehan stated no real differences from those of the other four coaches.

Linemen

Davis teaches his players that upper body strength is essential when blocking. The ability to give a great second effort on all blocks is valuable also. The other coaches all had no differences to talk about, except Henry, who wants his kids to keep contact when blocking.

Centers

All six coaches agree on the basic needs for a good center.

3. What is your defensive philosophy and why is it sound?

Davis starts by having a defense, which is completely sound. His defense is also able to cover all situations and the defensive rules for these situations are not so tough that players cannot learn them. Davis does not believe in standing a defensive lineup. He feels it makes the defense too soft and can be driven off the ball.

Allen feels defensively that there are five ways to score, while only three on offense. Defensively, you can score on an intercepted pass, punt return, or a recovered fumble and then you may also score on a safety or blocked punt. If either team can drive the opponent down to the goal line, the chance of scoring in one of the five methods mentioned above becomes a real threat and many times, they will win the ballgame.

To have the opposing team's offensive thrust backfire delivers a severe blow to its morale and could possibly lead to a collapse of the team.

McKee didn't really express any differences, but he did say it was important to strike hard on defense.

Sunset's Linehan is very basic in defensive techniques. His defenses are very honest but tough to score on. Sunset players spend many hours working on their defensive techniques because they know if they improve in practice, they will improve in their games.

Henry expressed a feeling of importance for total team defense. Linn had no real differences with the other coaches.

4. Please discuss what you would look for in personnel in the following defensive positions:
    a. defensive tackle
    b. linebacker
    c. defensive ends
    d. defensive backs

Davis felt they need a defensive tackles who are big in size because their teams play big offensive lines and they do not want their kids blown off the line of scrimmage. Allen stated no differences in his defensive tackles. McKee from Beaverton believes in standing his defensive lineup in order to avoid physical contact and have greater pursuit. Linehan, who is a great defensive coach, believes in a basic defense with touch tackles.

All six coaches agreed on the same ingredients for their linebackers.

Concerning defensive ends, all coaches agreed on the basic needs, along with McKee, but McKee added that his defensive ends play run two-thirds inside and one-third outside, unless it is an unusual offensive thrust.

In the area of defensive backs, all six coaches agreed except McKee, who felt that his kids need to be tall at this position in order to intercept the pass.

5. Why is the kicking game important and what do you look for in a good kicking game?

Davis feels it is important to break down the kicking game on film. Davis also feels that if you can win the kicking game and the offensive part of the game, or else the kicking game and the defensive part of the game, then you have won two out of the three areas needed for victory.

Allen has these differences. The type of offense you run, along with the kind of defense, all have a direct influence on your kicking game and how important it will be to you. If you have a power control offense, then it is very likely you would want a good punt and punt return team to keep the opponents as far away from your goal as possible. If you happen to get a successful punter, you can move the football many times, just by punting. If you can also get a kickoff man who can consistently kick the ball between the 10- to 23-yard lines low, you might just as well gamble on an onside kick. You can bet the opponent will run the ball back between the 30- to 45-yard lines. Unless you have a kicker who can kick the ball inside the 10-yard line. I am for using some other way or type of kickoff. The last thing is that we only let a few people work with our kickers so they won't have to think about too many things.

McKee from Beaverton feels if one of his kicks are blocked, it is a sin and should never happen. Linehan had no differences to express.

Linn and Henry all feel that getting the hidden yardage is important. Henry and Davis feel you must win two out of three: offense and defense, offense and kicking game, or defense and kicking game.

6. Give a general idea what is important in your football practices.

Davis feels that his warm-ups are important and when performing these warm-ups, being relaxed is important. He feels this is the best way to warm up his offensive personnel.

Linn, Allen, and Henry had no real differences in their practice techniques. McKee had only one difference and that was that his players need a short time every practice to talk. Linehan was in agreement with the other coaches. He did say, however, that they try and sell practice to their players.

7. What are your attitudes toward the following – Training?

Davis feels he likes to treat his players like men at the college level. Allen sincerely felt his players should help enforce the rules set up for training by the team. McKee teaches a great amount of loyalty. Linehan had nothing to add in his interview concerning training. Linn and Henry had nothing to add either.

8. What are your attitudes toward the following – Injuries?

All six coaches agreed they should know about all injuries so proper care could be given.

9. What are your attitudes toward the following – Relationships with Players?

Davis did not have any differences relating to the other coaches and their ideas on relationships with players. All coaches agreed that to do as much as possible for their players was very important and all felt it was important to be close with them in order to guide them properly. Also, to be firm, but fair was stressed.

10. What are your attitudes toward the following – Scouting?

All coaches agreed that films were best in finding out about their opponents. They did not have any differences of opinion.

CHAPTER 5
Summary, Conclusions, Recommendations

Summary

Of the five chapters in this study, chapter 1 introduces the problems of describing and analyzing the coaching philosophies of football coaches in Oregon. Chapter 2 reviews six personal interviews taken from Oregon coaches. Chapter 3 analyzes what the six coaches had in common. Chapter 4 analyzes what the six coaches did differently in their programs. Chapter 5 presents a summary, the conclusion, and the recommendations.

The purpose of this study was to describe and analyze the coaching philosophies of football coaches in Oregon. After thoroughly understanding each of the philosophies, the investigator prepared a comparison and summation of what these philosophies had in common.

Conclusion

After analyzing the interviews with the six coaches, the investigator formed the following conclusions relating to similarities. If a football coach is going to be successful, he must realize certain basic needs for his teams.

In question 1, we realize very quickly the basics of a good offensive philosophy. All seven coaches stressed the importance of an offensive philosophy fitting in with the total scheme. If the offense does not fit together with a particular defense or kicking game, an imbalance is then created and the outcome of the football games will not be the same.

Questions 2 and 4 dealt with offensive and defensive personnel being able to perform certain functions and have given strengths in the areas needed to play their particular position. For example, a back must have great speed and good balance. Linemen must be quick. An offensive player must be able to catch the football. All these needs are basic and essential.

Question 3 deals with the defensive philosophies of the coaches. Again, the importance is a sound approach to what defensive scheme you are going to use. Along with the basics of defense, such as pursuit, good tackling, and courage, the kicking game is discussed in question 5. The importance of this phase concerning football play cannot be emphasized enough. When all else fails in defensive play or offensive play, the kicking game can actually win for you. Your team can move the football the length of the field just by having a good punter and field goal kicker. A good kickoff man will drive the ball deep into enemy territory and deliver a severe blow to the opposition and make it that much harder for them to score.

In question 6, where football practices were analyzed, these conclusions were made. All football practices must be organized and function at a high level all the time. To maintain this level, practices must not be too long or too short. Drills must relate to football situations and be of short duration. Hitting should be done in football games and held down to a minimum in practice. All practices should be broken down and analyzed constantly to realize their true value.

Questions 7 through 10 provided some valuable thoughts all teams should set rules and guidelines to follow concerning the team and individual team members. Bad habits such as smoking and drinking are frowned upon.

Injuries are important to know about for the players' present needs, and for seasons to come. The best possible doctors should be available to work with players. Players should, by no means, be able to play if injured.

Scouting is very valuable in understanding your opponents. The best method of scouting is to film the game and then break this film down. It is also important to see your opponent in person.

Relationships with players are good and valuable to the parents as well as to the coach. He is able to communicate with his players in a close manner that his parents might not be able to achieve. It is a coach's job to help.

Recommendations to Others Who Study This Topic

From the findings and conclusions, the following recommendations are made:

1. The questions of this study were too general and need to be more specific.
2. The study should contain a larger sample of coaches and fewer, more specific questions.
3. The investigator must be sure and specify to the coaches interviewed the area to be covered.

Recommendations to Football Coaches

1. All coaches should be aware of the needs or foundations of each area concerning football coaching.
2. Not always will you find the perfect football player on your team. Nobodies can become superstars.
3. Every coach you will find different in certain areas, but they all have the same basic foundations for football.
4. Most coaches specialize in offense, defense, or the kicking game. Not many coaches specialize in all these areas, but do know the basic foundations needed for the total game.

SELECTED REFERENCES

1. Allen, John, Interview. Jesuit High School Head Football Coach, Beaverton, Oregon.

2. Davis, Darrel "Mouse," Head Football Coach, Portland State University, Portland, Oregon, Interview.

3. Henry, Ted, Offensive Coordinator, Linfield College, McMinnville, Oregon, Interview.

4. Linehan, Coach, Football Coach, Sunset High School, Beaverton, Oregon, Interview.

5. Lombardi, Vince, <u>Vince Lombardi on Football</u>, New York Graphic Society, Ltd., 1973, pp. 10–13.

6. inn, John, Football Coach, Beaverton High School, Beaverton, Oregon, Interview.

7. McKay, John, <u>Football Coaching</u>, Rolad Driess Company, New York, H. John McKay, University of Southern California, 1966, pp. 32–34.

8. McKee, Wayne, Football Coach, Beaverton High School, Beaverton, Oregon, Interview.+

CHAPTER 6

Coach Geigle's Thoughts

I thought it would be a good time to give readers my responses to the ten questions after playing and coaching football for over fifty years. I not only wanted to answer the question for my readers but also for myself so I wouldn't forget the many lessons I've learned from some of the best coaches in Oregon.

Question No. 1

1. What is your offensive philosophy and why do you feel it so effective?

My belief is that football is fundamentally a combative sport. Having said that, I believe football players need to be determined to win and consistent in playing a football game. My philosophy is to run the football between the tackles. By doing this, we make our opponents adjust to stop the inside run, which causes weaknesses in other parts of their defense. When we see the adjustment to stop the run inside, then we adjust and start running the ball outside. When we have gained success inside and outside moving the football, then our play action passes become effective and finally we start throwing the ball deep using our drop back pass. First and foremost, we run the ball. I also believe running the football sends a message to linemen to man up and get the job done. By running the football, we control clock and take away our opponents' ability to score a lot of points.

Question No. 2

2. Please discuss what you would look for in the areas concerning different offensive personnel and techniques of offensive personnel.

Tight Ends

Tight ends need to be tall and strong. They must be able to block big defensive linemen and linebackers as well as run good pass patterns and then have the ability to catch the football. I look for that tough, durable quality. I also think the tight end needs to be very deceptive when running pass routes and adjusting their stance for running plays.

Strongside Tackles

Strongside offensive tackles are our biggest and strongest offensive player. These players are not quite as fast but can still get down field even though they're big, strong, and tall. Our strongside tackles are the foundation of our offensive line and make important line calls. They are determined to defeat their opponent. They must have the ability to protect the quarterback on pass plays and block the defensive players down field on running plays.

Strongside Guard

Strongside guards must get off the ball quickly to block linebackers and are able to pull on sweeps and counter plays. They are strong and aggressive when blocking defensive linemen on sweeps. The strongside guard is a good pass blocker, able to read the inside pass rush and pick up stunts and does a good job protecting the quarterback. He is determined to defeat his opponent and he must be a good drive blocker.

Center

Centers are smart and most of all consistent. The center must snap the ball time after time without a mistake. He must be able to hike the football fast enough to get down field and block linebackers. He shows leadership and consistency and draws respect from the other players. It would be great if he had some height but not mandatory. The center must be a good pass blocker and protect the quarterback.

Weakside guard

Weakside guards are smaller and faster than the strongside guard. They are fast enough to block down on the nose guard or backside linebacker on running plays. Even though weakside guards are smaller, make no mistake, they are determined to defeat their opponent. They are expected to control the defensive linemen and protect the quarterback.

Weakside Tackle

When looking for a weakside tackle, I know he will not be quite as strong as the strongside tackle, but he will be quicker. His job is to seal off the backside on running plays and protect the outside rush on passing plays. He is aggressive and is a competitor on the field.

Split Ends

Split ends are able to catch the ball first, run second, and block down field third. They must have the speed and ability to fake out the defender. The split end must make key catches in a football game, which is crucial to winning. He will have great hands and pass catching technique. Spit ends spend many extra hours practicing timing routes with the quarterback. They are normally tall, fast, and have the ability to go up in the air and get the ball.

Tailback

The tailback should be our most talented ball carrier. He will have the speed to go outside and the toughness to run the ball inside on running plays. He has a natural instinct and ability to carry the football and a burning desire to score touchdowns. He also possesses the ability to catch passes and at times throw the football.

Fullback

Our fullbacks are big, strong, and quick to hit the hole. They must love to run the football and would rather take on the tackler than go around him. They carry the football on running plays with a wrecking ball mentality and will run over anyone who gets in their way. The fullback's number one job is to block for the tailback and then protect the quarterback on pass plays.

Slotback

The slotback is our speedster. He is smaller and lines up outside the weakside tackle and goes in motion to confuse the defense. He carries the football on reverses and catches the ball on passes.

Sometimes he will be asked to block on the inside running game. He plays with a competitive attitude and is lightning fast.

Quarterback

When looking for a quarterback, a number of qualities are needed. We would like the quarterback to be a ball handler first, a passer second, and a runner third. He possesses leadership, a desire to win, and the ability to move the football down the field. He is smart, poised, and plays at a high level in games and is admired by his teammates. The quarterback should have the ability to throw the ball down the football field with accuracy.

Question No. 3

3. What is your defensive philosophy and why is it sound?

Looking at defense, I've always liked the 5-2 because I believe it teaches players how to read the offense. There is no question that over the years my defenses have been very aggressive. I take a lot of chances sending different players to attack the quarterback and stop the play before it develops. I think there's a time to read the offense and there's a time to go after them in a game. I will do both. I will also try to disrupt the offensive line blocking by shifting my defense around. It not where you line up; it's where you end up that counts Right?

Question No. 4

4. Please discuss what you look for in the following positions on defense.

Defensive tackles are big, fast, and strong. They have gap responsibility and outside containment rushing on the pass plays. They should never be driven backward off the line of scrimmage.

The strongside tackle helps to stop the running game. They are relentless getting to the ball carrier on running plays or the quarterback on pass plays. Their techniques on pass rush includes the bull rush, the spin technique, and the swim. They use their height to raise their arms and knock down a quarterbacks pass attempt.

Linebackers

Linebackers line up five yards off the line of scrimmage. When the ball is hiked, they read their keys. If they read run, they come up to meet the blocker, then shuck him and tackle the ball carrier. If they read pass, they cover their pass responsibility. Linebackers are serious strikers, very quick, and compete at a high level. They understand the defense and are relentless in their pursuit of the ball carrier.

Defensive Ends

Defensive ends must never let the run get outside or turn the corner. Their number one job is to secure the outside run and close down the option. Defensive end are big, strong, and very quick. They are able to meet the blocker and destroy the running play before it develops. They have outside rush and containment responsibility on pass plays and must get their hands up to knock down quarterback's pass attempts. The defensive end needs to look for and destroy the reverse. He is a fierce competitor and relentless in his pursuit.

Defensive Backs

The defensive back never gets beat deep. The corners must be able to read pass first and then fill on the run. Defensive backs are smart and make key plays and interceptions in football games.

They must be good at blitzing and knowing their coverages. They are hitters when tackling and have a nose for intercepting the football.

Question No. 5

5. Why is the kicking game important and what do you look for in a good kicking game?

I've seen many football teams take the field and lose football games because they can't punt, kickoff, kick an extra point, or kick a field goal. The kicking game is very important to moving the football by driving your opponent back on a long punt or kickoff and giving you great field position and a serious advantage. We always look for players that will sell out by getting down field, perusing the football, and making the tackle or creating a fumble. We want to look for players that are consistent, and we have a good idea how far they can kick or return the football. We try to make the kicking game one more part of the football game we win.

Question No. 6

6. General idea what is important in your football practices.

Accountability is a serious part of my football practices. Players need to get better playing football and just like taking a quiz in school, they need to show that they're improving. I like to give the offense a situation and see what they can do with it and the same with defense, and if they don't do well, there's always a consequence. At the same time the practice drills need to be fun and competitive at the right time. I believe when a player does something well, the whole state should know it. Players love to hear their name and in my practice, if you do it right, it become a real moment you won't forget. I also feel writing practice plans for every practice is important to understand where you have been and where you're going, what's working, and what's not working. Last, I want my coaches coaching, not standing around talking about last year's fishing trip. I also don't believe in yelling at a player in front of the team or anyone else for that matter. I will, however, light a fire underneath the team's butt, as a group, to let them know their effort is unacceptable.

Question No. 7-10

What are your attitudes toward the following:

7. Training

Rules for misbehavior, for example, need to have serious consequences. Coaches need to explain the rules and make sure the players and parents understand that they can be removed from the team. On parent night, a real discussion with players' parents and players hearing the rules for misbehavior, and the signing of a contract by players and parents acknowledging what will happen if caught.

8. Injuries

We want to know about all injuries. We never want to put a player's health at risk to win a football game.

9. Relationship with players

Players need to understand that you care about them and you will do everything you can to give them a great moment in football. Your relationship with your player sets the tone for a positive or negative atmosphere. I will help my players any way I can as their football coach and mentor.

10. Scouting

I believe breaking down videos of opponents with the coaching
staff. Sending a coach to scout the team while they play a game.
It helps if it's a game the week before we play. It helps to get a feel
for who they are.

CHAPTER 7
The Story Of Chalk Talk

The Frog on the Track (late Summer 1971)

The first day that we reported for football practice at Linfield college, we all headed up into the bleachers at the college stadium to wait for coach Rutchman to give us the preseason speech.

While I was sitting in the cool morning air, I looked to my left and walking toward us on the track was a new freshman from Jesuit High School by the name of Steve Barsottie.

Steve had played defensive end for the Crusaders (Jesuit) and we found out very quickly that he was a little crazy.

I guess Steve wanted to make a quick statement to all the players sitting in the stands. We all watched as Steve approached and spied a frog that was hopping across the track in front of his path.

Without missing a step, with a quick swipe of his hand, Barsottie snatched up the frog. Without hesitating, he put the frog's head in his mouth and bitt it off, spitting the head out on the track in front of him.

He then threw the remains of the frog over on the grass, smiled at us and took a seat. I couldn't believe what I had witnessed and knew this guy was different from all the rest.

In 1971, we didn't think too much about what a kid like this was doing, biting the head off a frog. We were all kids and sometimes young men do things that may not be regarded as appropriate. In hindsight, it was an appalling act of cuelty... but Barsottie really was great kid. At 19, however, he was a kid. His character, as he matured, proved to be exemplary and we all admired him for the guy he really was, without the show-off actions of this first encounter.

Steve went on to be the starting defensive end for the Linfield Wildcats and went on, also, to become an All American and a great guy. His only problem was in the afternoons. When he showed up for practice, he couldn't keep his eyes open for chalk talk.

One day, Coach Rutchman got after Steve for dozing off while Coach had his back turned, drawing plays on the black-board. This particular day, Steve didn't want to get in trouble for dozing so he hung the back of his football jersey on a coat hook behind himself to hold his head up, so it would look like he was awake and paying attention. The only problem was our other defensive end, Jay Buse, would also doze off.

When Rutchman saw both players sleeping, he picked up a large, silver, garbage can that was nearby, lifted it up over his head with a crazed look in his eyes, ran over and slammed it down in front of both players.

Buse was so startled, his eyes flew open wide as he threw his elbow back against the wall behind him, knocking a hole the size of a basketball in the wall where his elbow landed. Barrsottie fell to the floor, letting out a terrifying yell and ripping the coat hook out of the wall, which had held him up, then with a frightened look on his face, just sat on the floor, starring at Coach Rutchman.

The room got real quite and all of us focused on Coach Rutchman to see what would happen next. There was a long silence that seemed to go on forever and then everyone burst into laughter, realizing that Coach was smiling and loving every moment of the theatrics that was his specialty. Everyone knew that Coach was just trying to get our attention because when he was really mad, a vein in his neck would bulge out. There was no vein this day. He was a great coach and teacher for a bunch of guys who were young and impressionable. He seldom let the seriousness of winning and losing, interfere with the humanity of the sport.

The rest of the season, when walking into the locker room, we always saw the patch on the wall where Buse had demonstrated his mighty power, Barrsottie had been frightened to his knees and the coat hook was no longer there. Both players will never be forgotten and always be remembered for their unique personalities and their lack of being able to stay awake.

A Boy Named Joe: Why I Coached Football

This is about a boy named Joe. Joe came from a family with four, very large sons. Joe's dad was six foot seven inches and a mountain of a man. Joe's brothers Pete, Stan, and Willie were just like their father—big, strong, and fast. All three boys played college and then pro football. When Joe became one of my students in the ninth grade, he wanted to be like his big brothers and play football. Joe had a learning disability but made up for it with his sense of humor and enthusiasm.

During the school year, Joe helped me with a fundraiser by putting on a haunted house. We set up a fake operation in the boys'

PE dressing room in the teachers' office. Joe played a doctor operating on someone who was lying on an operating table under blue lights. He used hamburger as bloody guts and had also made a recording of a heartbeat that lasted an hour, using his own voice for the sound effects. He played the heartbeat as people walked by and looked through the window, watching him operate. Then he would slowly turn and look at them and walk toward the door to open it as if to grab one of them like a mad scientist. It looked like the real thing. The haunted house made over two thousand dollars that night, and Joe was the big hit.

Joe's learning handicap prompted a tough discussion on whether it was safe for him to play football. As the head football coach, I could see the sadness that Joe was feeling by being told he couldn't play. At that time, we had two ninth-grade football teams. One team was made up of bigger players and the other team was smaller players. We did this to make the games safer and more competitive. After getting to know Joe, even though he was a tall kid with his disability, he would fit right in with the smaller team. Getting permission for him to play was not easy. Explaining to the staff why Joe should have a chance to be like his brothers wasn't easy.

When I finally had convinced the staff to allow Joe to try out for the team and was able to tell him; his eyes lit up and he walked around the school proud that he was going to be a football player. When practice started, I kept a close eye on Joe and made sure he was practicing with players close to his ability. The first time Joe was knocked down in a blocking drill, he started to cry. He just lay there on the ground weeping. I told all the players to move ten yards downfield and continued the drill. I told Joe when he was done crying that the team would be downfield and get up and get back in line. I also told him, "Welcome to football." After a while, I watched as he got to his feet and got back in line for the drill. When it was his turn again, he got knocked down. Again he started to cry again, so I moved the team, this time not saying a word. I was letting Joe decide whether he was going to play football or not. Joe got up and got back in line and was ready, once again, for his turn. This time, I told Joe that he needed to knock the whoop-tee-do out of the other player. You could see the determination in Joe's eyes. When the ball was hiked and the two players came together, Joe drove his opponent down the field, ten yards. The other players went crazy, cheering Joe on then surrounding him, patting him on the back, and telling him what a great job he had done. Joe was smiling from ear to ear. He never cried again. Joe went on to be the starting right tackle for the lightweight team and had a wonderful season. Joe was voted the most inspirational player by his teammates. He never played football again after that year, but we all knew it had changed him forever. Joe's family thanked me for all I had done. In the spring Joe became my baseball equipment manager and did a tremendous job, always wearing a big smile. I loved that guy!

Coach Sets The Pace

Last summer, I was sitting in the bleachers at Mountainside High School in Beaverton, Oregon, watching the new football coach run his players through their practice. I was there to support my grandson, Landon Sherman, in his attempt to make the varsity team. I had watched Landon through the years, starting out when he was just a little guy. From the moment he started playing he loved the game of football and enjoyed competing and being part of a team.

Sitting there, I watched as the new coach pushed his players to work hard; putting pressure on them, breaking from the huddle, running up to the the line of scrimmage, then qickly hiking the football. He was teaching his players that doing things at a faster tempo creates a winning edge, helps with conditioning and presents an atmosphere of hustle. As I continued to watch, it was pretty evident that you did what the coach wanted and earned the right to play or you rode the bench. There were no free rides on this team, everyone pulled their weight. I also saw that if a player made an honest mistake, he was immediatly surrounded by the other players, who made sure he felt a wave of positive support, letting him know to shake it off.

I leaned back on the bench with the warm rays of the sun hitting my face and admired the attention to detail in drills and watched the coaches ability to run the show. I knew very quickly he was a seasoned educator and was born to coach. His assistant coaches gave him the respect he deserved and listened to his every word, knowing that his many years of experience were earned. As the head coach, he was here to lead these young athletes and their new high school to victory. We all felt he was the right pick and a great addition to Mountainside High School. He had brought his wisdom of football from years of experience, winning and losing. His philosophy was ingrained into all his high school teams from lessons learned by performing hundreds of hours of practice, meetings, watching film and playing games on friday nights. I was very pleased that my grandson was having this man in his young life.

Being a retired coach myself, I knew this coach knew the secrets of winning, having won the high school state title at Silverton High school in Silverton Oregon before coming to Mountainside.

While sitting there, I had plenty of time, watching practice and thinking back about my days as a coach and teacher and how over the years I had gained wisdom and experience in coaching. I then, focused on the field looking down at coach. I watched this seasoned leader and smiled. This guy had my respect. He had earned the right of passage and earned the right to make the important football decisions. This leader had been in hundreds of situations and drew from his experiences knowing what to do, what works and what doesn't.

It's pretty easy for me, as a retired coach, sitting there on those hard metal bleechers to appreciate the wisdom being used down on the field. I started thinking about the world today and how we're trying to pass that wisdom on to a future generation. It seems in this fast paced world, many people want to lead without having learned the tough lessons that time can teach us. I've seen and met many who call themselves leaders after finding an early entry into a leadership role and wanting just to make their mark and achieve recognition. I've witnessed these leaders and their lack of ability to handle people and serious situations. They have a suitcase full of new ideas that haven't been thought out, but sound good. Then using their voice, telling people what they want to hear while looking for instant creditablity, attention and fame. These unseasoned leaders push their way into leadership and truly believe they have arrived, then quickly get in over their heads and find out they don't have wisdom or experience to draw from. The impact of these type of leaders over time, can keep us from doing things right, then clouding are vision, making us forget how we got here the first place. Smart leaders who have seen change, welcome new ideas, but have also seen many ideas come and go. They realize that making a change can be both rewarding and costly at the same time. Seasoned leaders know too many changes too quickly can lead to loss of direction and confusion and bring about a negative result. Wisdom tells us we need to use common sense and pay attention to our leaders.

Change comes from good decisions over time, to achieve good results.

Taking one last look from high in the bleechers, I look down at the field...practice is now coming to and end and it's been a good day. Down on the field the team is starting to look pretty good and we all know why. Our head coach is a great leader and it seems wherever he goes the sun shines brightly. His football program has evolved over the years without too many changes to a football philosophy that has served him well. My granson's in good hands!! GO MAVRICKS!!

PS

The football season is over now and the Mountainside Mavricks, with 8 wins and 4 losses, made it to the playoffs. Not only did they make it to the playoffs, but they knocked off the number one rated team in the state, the Tigard Tigers, 34-31, in an exciting overtime finish that will go down in Oregon High School history. Never has a number 16 rated team knocked off a number one rated team in the history of Oregon high school football. As of this moment, they have not won the state title, but there is always next year. Landon Sherman #12 made 3rd Team, all Metro and is looking forward to his next season as a Mavrick with Coach Mannion at the helm. As a grandfather, I sit here very proud of my grandson and the team for going the distance and Coach Mannion and his staff for the fine job this year!

Coach Geigle

ABOUT THE AUTHOR

Larry Geigle is a retired health and physical education teacher, athletic director, assistant principal, and football/baseball coach. He is also a grandfather, father, husband, and Vietnam veteran who lives in Lincoln City, Oregon, with his wife.

Larry attended Linfield College, where he earned a bachelor of science in health and physical education. He also has a master's degree in education from Linfield College. Larry also received his administrative license from Portland State University. His book covers coaching philosophies from over forty years of coaching football.

ABOUT THE BOOK

The purpose of this study was to describe and analyze the coaching philosophies of football coaches in Oregon. After thoroughly understanding each of the philosophies, the investigator prepared a comparison and summation of what these philosophies had in common.

Of the five chapters in this study, chapter 1 introduces the problems of describing and analyzing the coaching philosophies of football coaches in Oregon. Chapter 2 reviews seven personal interviews taken from Oregon coaches. Chapter 3 analyzes what the seven coaches had in common. Chapter 4 analyzes what the seven coaches did differently in their programs. Chapter 5 presents a summary, the conclusion, and the recommendations.

Printed in the USA
CPSIA information can be obtained
at www.ICGtesting.com
CBHW060045231124
17755CB00012B/104